Collins *Little book of*

SCRABBLE

BRAND Crossword Game

trickster

Barry Grossman

HarperCollins Publishers
Westerhill Road
Bishopbriggs
Glasgow
G64 2QT

First edition 2011

Reprint 10 9 8 7 6 5 4 3 2 1 0

© HarperCollins Publishers 2011

ISBN 978-0-00-744313-0

SCRABBLE® and associated
trademarks and trade dress are
owned by, and used under licence
from, Mattel, Inc. SCRABBLE is a
registered trademark of J.W. Spear &
Sons Limited, a subsidiary of Mattel,
Inc. © 2011 Mattel, Inc.

All Rights Reserved.

Collins ® is a registered trademark
of HarperCollins Publishers Limited

www.collinslanguage.com

A catalogue record for this book is
available from the British Library

Typeset by Davidson Publishing
Solutions, Glasgow

Printed and bound at Leo Paper
Products Ltd

Editorial Consultant
Philip Nelkon

Editor
Freddy Chick

For the Publisher
Lucy Cooper
Kerry Ferguson
Elaine Higgleton

Contents

Scrabble Basics

This book will help you enjoy playing *Scrabble Trickster*, the new version of Scrabble that lets you break all the rules. Play your trick cards right and you can beat the best.

We should begin though by saying a little about the traditional version of the game and answering some of the fundamental Scrabble questions.

Can short words be as useful as long ones? Yes! Can you really get a 50-point bonus by playing seven letters? Yes! Can you get high scores with hard letters like Q and Z? Yes! And, as you will learn, this is all truer than ever in *Scrabble Trickster* where the trick cards let you run wild.

Anyone can improve by learning a few handy hints. You don't have to be young, you don't have to be a university professor, and *you don't even have to speak English* (as you'll see from the

page headed *World Scrabble* later in the book). So let's try to answer a few of your questions about Scrabble before we move on to the joys of *Trickster*.

Should I always go for the highest score?

No. You should certainly always bear in mind what score you can get from a particular move, and the highest score will often be the best move to make. But not always.

Here are some examples of highest-scoring moves which may not be the best move:

1. If you have only or mainly one-point tiles, with a good vowel-consonant balance, you may well be close to a 50-point bonus for playing all seven letters. With a rack of

   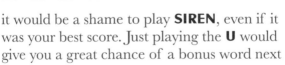

   it would be a shame to play **SIREN**, even if it was your best score. Just playing the **U** would give you a great chance of a bonus word next turn.

2. If you are ahead, block off the places where your opponents could score highly to get back

in the game. Look especially for rows or columns where *they* might get a bonus word and put something there yourself to block.

3. Even if you can't leave yourself with letters that look bonus-friendly, try to play something that leaves you with a good balance of consonants and vowels.

What are these letters and numbers round the board?

Modern Scrabble boards, and all *Scrabble Trickster* sets, have the letters A-O printed down the left-hand side of the board and the numbers 1-15 along the top.

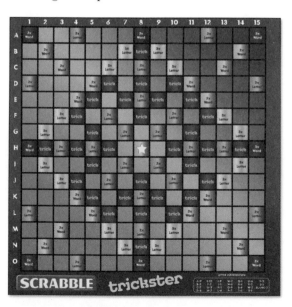

Every square on the board can then be identified by its letter and number. So the square in row G, column 9, can be referred to as G9. The central, starred square (which, being pink, is a Double Word square) is H8.

If the word **CAT** is played with the C on the M4 square, we say it is played at M4. Even if the **C** was already on the board from a previous move, so no tile is actually placed on M4 in the move in question, we still say it is played at M4.

Why do I always get all vowels?

Many players bemoan their luck at not being able to "balance their rack" – in other words, never seeming to have a good mix of vowels and consonants. In particular, a rack often seems to deteriorate into a mass of vowels.

Some people always look to use their highest-scoring letters first, to get the highest score possible for that move. (Not always a good plan, as we've already seen.) As the vowels are all worth one point, they may concentrate on playing higher-scoring consonants, leaving an excess of vowels on their rack. Then, if they pick more vowels, they start to struggle.

Always aim to leave yourself with as good a balance as you can after playing a move – either the same number of vowels as consonants, or one or two more consonants than vowels.

If you get stuck with vowels, there are a few useful words that are worth knowing:

EUOUAE	AIDOI
EUOI	OIDIA
EAU	AIOLI
AUE	AINEE
AUA	OUIJA
AIA	ZOEAE

Strange though they may look, they are all acceptable. Most of them are from Greek, though you will be familiar with the ouija board.

Where can I find these useful words?

The official book used for club and tournament play in the UK is *Collins Official Scrabble Words*. As of January 2012 the new edition will come into use in tournaments and competitions.

A sister book, *Collins Official Scrabble Lists*, puts the words into learning lists rather than a straight alphabetical format. For instance, you get all the two-letter words together, the threes, and the fours. All sevens and eights are listed in a way that you can check whether the seven letters on your rack will yield a seven or eight-letter word. Obviously these are for checking after, not during the game. The book has dozens of other lists, fascinating in their content if at times a little daunting in their sheer numbers of words.

You can find out more about valid words (as well as all aspects of tournaments and clubs) by visiting the website of the Association of British Scrabble Players, absp.org.uk

How can I make bonus words?

In several places, this book will mention bonus words – getting a 50-point bonus by playing all seven letters for a seven or eight-letter word (or, rarely, nine letters or more, but let's not worry about that here).

Playing a couple of bonus words per game is what makes a top player. Those extra fifties really get your score moving and take your game into a whole different dimension.

The easiest way to get them is to realise that the one-point tiles – **LNRST** and the five vowels – are the commonest letters in English. So hold on to those letters when you get them, especially **NRST** and **AEI** and perhaps **O**. Of course you can't do this to the exclusion of all else – so try to keep scoring while you are moving your rack towards a bonus combination.

Learning some less common words like **OTARINE**, **GREISEN** and **ETESIAN**, as well as being able to recognize the likes of **INERTIA** and **JANITOR** and anagrams like **PAINTER/ REPAINT/PERTAIN** will soon move your game up a few notches.

Any other golden rules?

One more important point to consider is "board management".

Put simply, this means you should try not to give your opponent any gilt-edged opportunities for a high score next turn. For instance, putting a *vowel* next to a premium square, especially a Triple Letter or Triple Word, may allow your opponent a high score next turn. Try to avoid it.

poor play   good play

In this example, by avoiding placing the **A** next to the Triple Letter square, you prevent your opponent from scoring a possible 50-plus for **AX**, **EX** or **XU**.

So where you play is as important as what you play?

Definitely. You should be aware whether any move you make (or your opponent makes) is an *opener* (opening up areas of the board), a *blocker* (closing areas off), or neutral.

Take a look at this board:

At the moment, a word could be played in row B – perhaps a 7-letter word, if the space is free all the way along, by making **BRAIN**, **DRAIN**, **GRAIN** or **TRAIN**.

If you don't have **B**, **D**, **G** or **T**, you could open it up by playing like this:

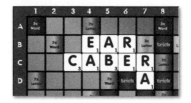

There are now lots of chances to play in row A, because so many letters go before **EA**, **AB** and **RE** to make three-letter words (all the vowels go before **RE**, as well as P). That makes it a very dangerous move, and you should only do it if you are sure your opponent cannot take advantage (perhaps having used a "Look at Opponent's rack" card in *Trickster*).

On the other hand, a simple blocking move
would be:

That simple F makes all the difference. Nothing
is now playable in the top row, and row B is very
difficult – something like **LOFTIEST** would be
possible but you would be very unlucky if an
opponent was sitting with that (remember B7
still has to be B, D, G or T).

FE would be a good move if you were ahead
and wanted to block off the board, especially
the chances of a comeback bonus by your
opponent.

What are these two-letter words?

We've mentioned a couple of odd two-letter words already and it's these little gems that are the lifeblood of Scrabble. They let you play in awkward spaces and make some really cunning moves.

Your *Scrabble Trickster* set has a card containing the two-letter words, which you can look at in exchange for giving up a trick card. But why not try to learn them, then you won't have to give up a potentially valuable card? There are 123 listed on the two-letter word card (Scrabble clubs allow a 124th, **TI**).

In this example, **BANGERS** has been played for a 50-point bonus, also making **AH**, **NO**, **GU** and **ER**.

Anywhere else I should avoid playing?

It's always dangerous to place a tile in the top or bottom row, or left or right column, if this opens up a Triple Word square for your opponent.

If you've just made a word beginning with **E** in column 2, you have given your opponent a chance for an easy Triple Word, maybe with a high-scoring consonant on A4.

Admittedly, if your opponent can't take the chance, you might get it, or your opponent might feel forced to play a low-scoring blocking move. But remember that if you make the opening, your opponent gets the first chance to exploit it. If you are playing two or three people, the chances of your opening still being there when it gets back round to your turn are even slimmer.

How should I deal with 🄹, 🅀, 🅇 and 🅉?

JQXZ, sometimes known as the power tiles, score either eight (**J** and **X**) or ten (**Q** and **Z**), so they are not to be sniffed at. Try to learn a few of the shorter words containing each, which might help you fit one into a high-scoring position. The twos are especially useful:

JA	QI	ZO	EX	OX
JO	ZA	AX	XI	XU

Notice that the **X** goes with all five vowels, either before or after.

These words give a good flavour of the wide variety of sources of the English language. **JA** is from South Africa (yes), **JO** is Scottish (a sweetheart), **QI** Chinese (life force), while **ZA** is New York slang (pizza) and **ZO** Tibetan (a type of yak). **XI** is a Greek letter and **XU** a Vietnamese coin.

Always try to get at least double value for a **J**, **Q**, **X** or **Z**, while playing it in a way that prevents your opponent from getting much use out of it.

I like QI – any more like that?

QI is of course especially useful, as it allows you to use a **Q** without having a **U**. There is quite a handful of these **U**-less **Q** words, so it pays to be familiar with them. The shorter ones are:

QI	**FAQIR**
QAT	**NIQAB**
QADI	**QANAT**
QAID	**QIBLA**
QOPH	**QORMA**
WAQF	**TALAQ**
	TRANQ

All these words are nouns and can have an **S** added to them. Most of them are from Arabic, although **TRANQ** is US slang for a tranquilizer.

Every new edition of the *Collins Dictionary*, from which the Scrabble word list is mainly compiled, brings some new riches. The 2011 edition contains **QIN**, a Chinese stringed instrument and a must learn word for all Scrabble players.

What's different about Scrabble Trickster?

The *Scrabble Trickster* board is the familiar 15 x 15 shape, with Double Letter, Triple Letter, Double Word, and Triple Word squares, though some of these squares are not in the same position as they are on the standard Scrabble board.

However, as well as these premium squares, there are also 32 trick squares. Placing one of your tiles on a trick square allows you to play a trick card – and that's when the fun starts.

A trick card might let you steal a tile from an opponent, spell a word backwards, or even make yourself another blank by turning one of your tiles face down. There are 19 different trick cards altogether, and in the following pages we will look at them one by one, see how to make the best use of them, and give each one a mark out of ten according to how useful it is.

Get your Trick Cards Early

If you look at the *Scrabble Trickster* board, you will see that most of the trick squares are clustered around the centre of the board. So that means the easiest time to get them is early in the game, because the game starts in the centre.

Try to make sure you cover at least one trick square every time with your early plays. And remember you can get two or even three trick cards at one go if you cover two or three trick squares.

It is even possible to cover more than three trick squares in one play, especially by playing the "Play more than one word during your turn" card. You could then pick even more trick cards, but you can only keep three at a time, so you would have to discard something. But you would have given yourself a great chance of picking one or two of the best ones.

It is worth getting a bit of a smaller score in those early shots to make sure you get yourself a good selection of trick cards. After all, without the trick cards, *Scrabble Trickster* isn't *Scrabble Trickster* at all!

Add ten points to your score

**You get to add ten
And maybe triple it then**

trick

Add 10 points to your score.

Points are added before doubling or tripling a word score.

USEFULNESS (OUT OF 10): 5

The important thing to notice here is that the points are added **before** doubling or tripling a word score. So play this card when you've just covered a double, or even better a triple, word score; that way your extra ten becomes an extra 20 or 30.

Blank tile is worth five points

**It can be any letter,
But to score with it's better.**

trick

Blank tile
is worth
5 points.

USEFULNESS: 4

Out?lanking the Opposition

This card is all well and good – as long as you pick a blank. With only two blanks in the set, you may never get the chance to use it, especially if three or four of you are playing.

Once both the blanks are played, this card is useless, so make sure that, if the blanks are both on the board, you get rid of it if you have more than three. (You can only have up to three trick cards at one time.)

If you do get the chance to play it, you should of course try to get it on a double or triple letter square, or get your word on a premium word square – that way you could get an extra 30 points. For instance:

Playing **DRANK** here, with the blank as a K, and playing your trick card, would score you 36. But changing to **GRAND**, with the blank as a G, gets you 45 – by playing the blank on a Double Letter score your five points are doubled, then the whole word score is tripled.

Cancel another player's card

**This card is the best,
For it trumps all the rest.**

This is a **very** useful card. Since you can use it to cancel out a powerful card played by another player, it has to be as powerful as any of them.

It follows then that you shouldn't use it willy-nilly. Wait for an opponent to get a really good score of their own with a card – and then pounce.

Perhaps your opponent has played the "Spell a word backwards" card. If they have only scored 10 or 15 points with it, let it go (unless perhaps they have used it to play an awkward Q, so that you can use your card to make them pick it up again). But if they have used it to score 30 or 40, that's when you could strike.

Double word score

**A quick sneaky double
Puts opponents in trouble.**

trick

Double
Word
Score

USEFULNESS: 6

Not much to be added here, except to point out that if you make more than one word in a move, you choose which one gets doubled, so make sure you pick the highest-scoring one. Wait for a good score before playing this card – it's obviously better to double a word that scores 25 than to double a word that scores 11.

Exchange racks with another player

**Get rid of your rack,
Get a better one back.**

trick

Exchange racks,
tiles only, with
another player
before taking
your turn.

USEFULNESS: 6

Now this is an interesting one. Using it is a bit of a step into the unknown – you might swap racks with another player only to find theirs is worse than yours.

If it's the first round of the game, or your opponent has just played five, six or even seven tiles, what they will have on their rack will be close to a random pick from the bag, so it would be best not to swap racks with them. But if they have just played one or two tiles, they may be holding back good letters to try for a bonus, so that could be the time to strike with this card.

Even better would be if it was close to the end of the game, and you can see that some good tiles (especially the blanks, or at least one of them) have not been played yet. If you are only playing one opponent, he or she might well have those good tiles. So go for the exchange, as long as there aren't also awkward tiles like **Q**, **J** or **V** to come.

If you are playing more than one opponent when you get this card, and your own rack is unpromising, swap either with the person who has just played one or two tiles rather than six or seven, or with the person who is winning (to saddle them with your rotten letters), or just with the person you think is the best player, to make life difficult for them and because they are most likely to have built themselves a good rack of letters.

In this game, your rack is

You can see that the blanks have not been played, and there are a couple of Ss unaccounted for. All the big, awkward tiles have been played, apart from the Y you are holding. Note that someone has used the "Spell a Word Anywhere" card in the bottom right corner.

There are chances for a bonus, using the **S** at H15 or N12, or the P at C2. You could even get a nine-timer, a word covering two Triple Word squares. Can you see where?

The answer is that, with one **A** unplayed, it may be possible to play from H1-O1, turning **GAIN** into **AGAIN**. The nine letters left are actually **AEEISST** and the two blanks.

So change your rack and take your opponent's if you are holding the card. With even one blank, you might get **PASTIMES** at C2 for 63, **BEASTIES** at A15 for 74, or even **SATIATES** at H1 for 129.

Exchange and still play

If in doubt,
Chuck 'em out.

trick

Exchange any
number of your
tiles for new ones
from the tile
bag AND still
play a word.

USEFULNESS: 7

A handy card if you use it carefully. You may have got stuck with a completely hopeless rack like this:

or an unbalanced rack with six or seven vowels or six or seven consonants.

First of all, have a quick check to make sure the rack really is as bad as it looks. Even with the rack above, you might be able to play **VOW** (**JOW** is also allowed), or, with the right floating letter on the board, something like **QUIN**, **QUIT** or **JIVE**.

But if the situation is hopeless, this card comes into its own. You might want to keep **QU** from the rack above, or a high-scoring 2-letter word like **QI** or **JO**. But if there are blanks and s's still in the bag, it might be best to change all seven.

All Change?

What should you change from a vowel-heavy or consonant-heavy rack? Have a look at what has already been played. Are there words on the board with lots of consonants, like **NIGHT**, **BLINK** and **SCRATCH**? If so, there must be plenty of vowels to come, so keep a couple of your best consonants back if that's what you have. On the other hand, if the board has words like **IDEA**, **EERIE**, or those Scrabble-specialist words like **EUOI**, then you are likely to pick consonants so hold a couple of vowels back, especially an **E**.

Pirates are Common; Comfort Scarce

You might see that you have a rack like

C O M F O R P

and be tempted to change just the **P** in the hope of picking a **T** to make **COMFORT**. It's not a wise move to "go fishing" like this since if you don't pick the **T** (which you probably won't), you haven't improved your rack.

But if your rack reads

A E I R S T U

you might notice that *several* other letters would give you a 7-letter word if you change the **U** (**RETAINS** or **NASTIER** with an **N**, **PIRATES** or **PARTIES** with a **P**, **SATIRES** with an **S**, **SALTIER** or **REALIST** with an **L**, etc). So that is the time to change one tile – checking first that there is somewhere to play your 7-letter word if you do get it.

Look at another player's rack

**You're not being a sneak
If you have a quick peek.**

trick

Look at
another player's
rack of tiles.

USEFULNESS: 6

Another potentially useful card if it's used well. Let's say the bottom right-hand corner of the board looks like this:

Your rack consists of:

You would like to play **COURT** using the **U** on the board, scoring 26. But what if your opponent has an **S**, ready to grab the Triple Word Score you have opened by making **COURTS** and a word down the right-hand column? A glance at their rack will tell you all you need to know. If you have more than one opponent, look at the rack of whoever is winning (or whoever is second if you are winning).

Make a player lose a turn

Opponent looks smug?
This card pulls the rug.

trick

Make a player lose their turn.

This card must be played at the beginning of the opponent's turn.

USEFULNESS: 8

Again, this one's all about timing. The best times to play this card could be:

1. Near the end of the game. Not right at the end when players are playing off their last one or two tiles, as scores tend to be low at that stage, but perhaps when an opponent has their last chance to play a high-scoring bonus. And if there's only one place to play a bonus, you can then block it so they can't play there on their next move either.

2. If your opponent only played one or two tiles in their previous shot, they may be fishing for a bonus. Play your card and see if they gnash their teeth with frustration.

Tile usually worth one is worth ten

**Common letters score highly,
If you use this card slyly.**

trick

One tile usually worth 1 point is worth 10 points.

This change in point value applies to this turn only.

USEFULNESS: 7

Of course, this one is all about getting a one-pointer on a triple letter square, or in a word which covers a triple word. Look for those combinations of squares that can give a really high score from a ten-point tile – the tile itself on a premium letter square, and the whole word on a premium word square.

On this board, your opponent has played **GLOWER**, figuring correctly that there aren't many words with a **G** in second position, so it's hard to hit the triple word score on A1 – and especially hard to get a high-scoring tile on A4.

But using your card, you could play a simple word like **OGRE:** you claim ten for the **E**, which is doubled to 20, the whole word is tripled, and that's a massive 72 points.

How the letter values came about

Alfred Butts, the inventor of Scrabble, established the frequencies and points values for each letter by counting the number of times they each appeared on the front page of an edition of the New York Times. Nowadays one could easily access letter counts for a million words, or the whole dictionary, online, but such resources were not available to Mr Butts in those early days.

If we were to reinvent Scrabble today and come up with a new set of letter values, we might drastically reduce the **X** and **Z**, to perhaps six for the **X** and seven or eight for the **Z**. **H** is usually quite easy to score with and might be reduced from four to two or three.

Letters that might be increased are **L** and **U**, not much value for a point each and surely worth two. The **B**, I find, is more awkward than its *fellow three-pointers **C**, **M** and **P**, and is more on a par with four-pointers like **F** and **W**.*

*To be fair, I am a Scrabble wonk for whom words like **COZ**, **ZORI**, **ZEX**, **DIXI** and **LIMAX** are ingrained in my Scrabble vocabulary. For the more social player, perhaps old Alf got it just about right.*

Play a proper noun

**You could play QYRGHYZ,
If you can spell it, that is!**

trick

**Play a
proper noun.**

A proper noun
is a word that is
usually capitalised.

USEFULNESS: 5

This is the one which the newspapers got hold of a little while ago and came out with banner headlines that "they" were changing the rules of Scrabble and allowing proper names. Of course, "they" were doing no such thing, except in *Scrabble Trickster* and only when you have this card. The papers getting something wrong – imagine!

It's probably not even one of the most useful cards, especially as many words you might think of as proper names are in fact allowable words anyway. Personal names which are valid Scrabble words include:

JOHN   A general term for a man, especially in US

HENRY   A unit of inductance in physics

BARRY   A blunder

JESUS   A size of paper

SHEILA   A woman (Australian)

JEAN   A material

And there are place-names too:

BRAZIL A type of nut
SPAIN To wean a baby
BERLIN A type of carriage

This card will perhaps give you the chance to play a high-scoring tile in a good position. Here are some proper names containing the power tiles **J**, **Q**, **X**, and **Z**. Those marked with an asterisk * are valid words in normal play so you can play them without using your card.

It's Who You Know that Counts

Names with **J**

FIJI	JARROW	JOE*
FUJI*	JASON	JOHN*
JACK*	JAVA*	JON
JACKIE	JAYNE	JORDAN*
JACKY*	JEAN*	JOSH*
JACOB	JEDDAH	JOSS*
JAKE*	JEFF*	JUDAS*
JAMAL	JENNY*	JUDY*
JAMES*	JERRY*	JULIA
JAN	JESUS*	JULIE
JANE*	JILL*	JULIET
JANET	JIM	RAJ*
JAPAN*	JIMMY*	RAJIV
JARED	JO*	

Names with **Q**

IQBAL	QIN	QUEZON
QASIM	QING	TARIQ
QATAR	QOM	

Names with X

EXE	OXFORD*	XANTHE
EXETER	OXHEY	XAVIER
EXMOOR	ROXY	
MAX*	TEXAS*	

Names with Z

BRAZIL*	ZAK	ZENA
GAZA	ZARA	ZOE
LIZ	ZEKE	ZOG
QUEZON	ZELDA	ZULEIKA
ZACK*	ZEN	

The Fine Art of Name Dropping

And some 7- and 8-letter proper names that could be useful: **Geographical terms** (maximum of 1 tile worth more than one point)

AIRDRIE	CROATIA	PARISIAN
ALGERIA	ESTONIA	PRESTON
ALGIERS	IRELAND	SERBIAN
ASIATIC	ISRAELI	SIAMESE*
BRISTOL*	ITALIAN	SLOVENIA
BRITAIN	LATVIAN	SUDANESE
CARLISLE	NIGERIA	TUNISIA

Boys' names (maximum of 2 tiles worth more than one point)

BERNARD	GERVASE	STEPHEN
CHARLES	LEONARD	STEWART
CHARLIE*	MAURICE	TERENCE
FRANCIS	RUSSELL	
GABRIEL	STANLEY	

Girls' names (maximum of 2 tiles worth more than one point)

ADRIENNE	FRANCES	MAUREEN
ARIADNE	ISABELLA*	MELISSA
BERNICE	JASMINE*	NIGELLA*
CAROLINE	KATRINA	PAULINE
CORDELIA	KATRINE	ROSALIND
CORNELIA	KIRSTEN	SIDONIE
CRESSIDA	KIRSTIN	THERESA
DESIREE	MARGARET	VALERIE
DEIRDRE	MARLENE	VANESSA*
EUGENIA*	MARTINA	VERONICA*
EUGENIE	MARTINE	VICTORIA*

Quite why girls' names crop up so much more frequently than boys' in the 7- and 8-letter list is an interesting question. But whether they are boys, girls, countries, whatever, all these names are made up mainly of common letters so you may just be able to make one with the proper noun trick card (or without, if it's got an asterisk).

In case you are wondering what some of the words marked with an asterisk mean, here are a few of the most interesting ones:

ISABELLA dingy or drab
JACKY a sailor
JAPAN to coat with lacquer
JEAN a material (hence **JEANS**)
JESUS a size of paper
JORDAN a chamberpot
MAX an old word for gin
SIAMESE to join pipes together
TEXAS part of a steamboat
VANESSA a type of butterfly
VERONICA a herb
VICTORIA a large water lily
ZACK an Australian coin (slang)

'I christen thee ZIVARJEQ'

Obviously these lists are not exhaustive. Almost anything can be a surname, or, these days, a first name. Gone are the days when parents contented themselves with John and

Mary, as a glance at the births column in your newspaper will show. The proper name card could lead to a few family squabbles as to what exactly is a name, but it all adds to the fun.

Let your mind range far and wide when you're thinking of proper names. Names from far Eastern countries like China and Korea are often short – why not fit in **MAO**, **KIM** or even **NG**? Almost any part of the world can contribute something; thinking of Africa might remind you about **ZULU***, or North America could make you think of **SIOUX**. How about the Indian surname **VAZ** or ex-Albanian King **ZOG**, or a nice simple **DAI** or **IAN** might help you fit a word in. Sri Lanka, where, as Test cricket fans know, the typical surname runs to 12 letters or more, may be less useful, though feel free to play **MURALITHARAN** if you can get it.

Perhaps the most spectacular proper name you could come up with is **QYRGHYZ**, a nomadic people of Central Asia. So feel free to slot that one in if you've got the only **Q**, the only **Z**, both the **Y**'s, and the right trick card.

If you happen to find one of these names on your rack, but you haven't got the card, it's worth remembering that many of them have anagrams which are valid words. You could have the **PRONEST POSTERN** in **PRESTON**, be a **LADRONE** (robber) called **LEONARD**, tell **MARTINE** you like her **RAIMENT** in a **MINARET**, or even know a bit of a **STINKER** called **KIRSTEN**. (Sorry to all those Kirstens out there.)

World Scrabble

Where is English-language Scrabble played? You may think of Britain and Ireland, America, Canada, Australia, New Zealand, South Africa – the main English-speaking countries. And of course it is played in all those places.

But it's much more widespread than that. The 2011 World Championship will be played in Warsaw, and will have participants from 42 countries including Poland, Romania, France, Germany, Sweden, Saudi Arabia, Pakistan, Japan and Indonesia.

The Far East is particularly keen on the game. Malaysia, Thailand and the Philippines have it on school curriculums. Malaysia has hosted the World Championship and a Thai, Panupol Sujjayakorn, won it in 2003. What makes the achievement of these players all the more remarkable is that in most cases English is not *their native language, or at least not their first language. Everything is learned by rote.*

*At a tournament a couple of years ago, I played a young Romanian (this wasn't anywhere exotic – in fact, Coventry). Early in the game I played **FUME** – which he challenged. I confess I felt a bit smug, and wondered whether I should advise him to play in a lower division next time. A few moves later I played **AEGROTAT** (a type of university degree), which he accepted without blinking an eye. He had learned **AEGROTAT** as a "high-probability eight" (note that all its letters are one-point tiles except the **G**, which is worth two). He went on to win the game.*

Play more than one word in your turn

You play more than one word,
Though it sounds quite absurd.

trick

Play more
than one word
during your turn.

If you use all 7 letters
on your rack, you
do not score a
50 point bonus.

USEFULNESS: 8

One of the most useful cards in the pack. Note that you don't get the 50-point bonus for playing all seven tiles if you use this card. The best use of it could be to set yourself up for a high score, and know you can play it before anyone else gets the chance to block.

For example, look at this board (bottom left-hand corner):

Your rack:

That double-letter triple-word combination on row O looks tempting, especially with your high-scoring **X**. Ordinarily you couldn't take it yet as you are still one row away. Open it up (with, say, **AT** at N2) and an opponent will probably grab it before you get the chance.

But using this card, you could simply play **PA** down from M2, scoring 8, and follow that up with **CRUX** at O1, for a handsome 68. Then either play your remaining **ET** for a few more points, or hold onto them as the basis of a good rack for next time.

Score a previously used premium space

Re-use Triple Word square,
With this card it's quite fair.

trick

Score a previously used premium space.

USEFULNESS: 6

It's fairly obvious that playing this card to reuse a Triple Word square will generally give you the best value. Look for a reasonably high-scoring letter on a Triple Word square and a very ordinary word played onto it could bag you a hatful of points.

This is a card you want to pick later in the game rather than earlier, once some Triple Word squares have been reached. If you pick it too early, you may have to use it where you can rather than lose it altogether under the "no holding more than three trick cards" rule, depending on how useful your other cards are.

Spell a word anywhere

Play anywhere at all,
Increase your points haul.

trick

Spell a word
ANYWHERE
on the board.

USEFULNESS: 7

Every Scrabble player knows the heart-sinking feeling of having a lovely word, perhaps a seven-letter word, on the rack but nowhere to fit it on the board. This is the card to change all that.

It's easiest to use at the beginning of the game. Towards the end, when the board gets crowded, you might find you still can't place your word even using this card.

Of course, because the play expands out from the centre, it's likely to be in the corners that you'll be able to place your word with the card. And what do you find in the corners? Yes, those lovely Triple Word squares which are usually so much of an effort to reach. So play that "unplayable" bonus, and on a Triple Word score into the bargain. A very welcome card to pick.

Play it anywhere - but not just *anywhere*.

With this board, you have a rack of

and the Spell a Word Anywhere card. First of all, can you find a 7-letter word from the rack? There are three great ones. Try putting **RE** at the beginning or **ER** at the end.

Did you get them? The words in question are **RETIRAL**, **RETRIAL** and **TRAILER.** But there's nowhere to fit them in.

No problem. Use your card to play one of them through any Triple Word square. You should avoid *starting* from a triple Word square, as that could give an opponent a chance to add an S to your word, and get a big score of their own. For instance, if you play **RETIRAL** at H15, scoring 74, your opponent might play **AXLES** at O11 for 84 – not quite the object of the exercise as far as you are concerned.

Also, avoid putting a vowel next to a Triple Letter square, as that could likewise give your opponent the chance to put a high-scoring consonant there for a high score.

And bear in mind, if any spaces stretching between two Double Word squares are available, your word score would be multiplied by four – even better than a Triple Word score.

WRONG
Possible AXLES
or similar at O11

WRONG
Possible QAT
at H14 for 67

BETTER

If, instead of the **E**, you had the **J**, you could still take advantage of the card by playing **JAIL** at O12 or other places for 57.

So always hold this useful card back until you can get the best use from it, either by playing an otherwise unplayable bonus, or getting a high score with **J**, **Q**, **X** or **Z**.

Spell a word backwards

**To get more points by far,
Turn your rack into KCAR!**

trick

Spell
a word
backwards.

USEFULNESS: 6

A curious one. It should be a very useful card – after all, it doubles the number of available words at a stroke. Well, not quite double, since some words can be spelt backwards already, like **ON/NO** and **DESSERTS/STRESSED.** But it certainly adds many, many more words.

Yet it could be an awkward one to use. We are just not used to thinking of words backwards; it will take quite a mental leap to use this card.

The best use could be to get a high-scoring tile on a Premium Letter square. **ZOO** with the second **O** on a Triple Letter scores 14. But **OOZ** in the same position gets 32. (Then it could be extended to **OOZE** in a subsequent move.)

Sometimes a good word may not be playable on the board forwards, but could slot in backwards. Perhaps there is a word on the top row, which you can add an S to and play down from. If you had a nice seven-letter word like **ENSURES** on your rack, you couldn't play it; but you could use this card to fit in **SERUSNE**.

It may be worth remembering that there are very few words beginning with **X** or ending with **J**, **Q** or **V**. But with this card, new worlds open up for you – enjoy yourself making **XOB**, **PMUJ**, **TIUQ** or **ALLIV**. There are words ending in **Z** but many of them end in **ZZ**, so can't be played without a blank. But now you can go for **PIZ** or **ARBEZ**.

Freaky Physics Family

Incidentally there is a very strange little family of words that can be read backwards or forwards. They come from the study of physics – no, don't go, this isn't too difficult. We start with these three words

OHM   a unit of resistance
FARAD a unit of capacitance
HENRY a unit of inductance

But all these words can also exist backwards, as reciprocal values of the original word. So **MHO**, **DARAF** and **YRNEH** are all playable. Here endeth the science lesson – I'm already in way over my head, and I'm guessing you might be as well.

Just be warned this doesn't work with all measurements from physics. You can't turn **WATT** into **TTAW** or **AMP** into **PMA** – unless, of course, you are holding the "Spell a word backwards" card.

Quadruple score on small words

**This card isn't so hot,
It won't score you a lot.**

trick

Spell one of the
following words
for quadruple the
points shown
on the tiles:
AT, AS, IS, OR,
TO, AN, IT, SO

USEFULNESS: 2

This card allows you to play **AT**, **AS**, **IS**, **OR**, **TO**, **AN**, **IT** or **SO** for quadruple points. So if the word was on a Triple Word square and scored six, with this card it would score 24.

Now, the deep-level analysis of *Scrabble Trickster* is still in the early stages. The Deep Blue supercomputer, fresh from its triumph over Mr Kasparov on the virtual chess board, has not yet been brought to bear. Much research remains to be done.

But I'm willing to bet that when the final, definitive volume is written, this card will turn out to be the most useless waste of 15 square centimetres of paper in the box.

These words will normally score only a couple of points. Even quadrupling them gives you a distinctly underwhelming score. Yes, you could get one on a Triple Word, but what are you doing playing a word like that on a Triple Word square anyway? Triple Word squares are for long or high-scoring words.

The only advice with this card has to be: if you have four cards and so have to get rid of one, make it this one.

Steal a tile from an opponent

**You can steal a tile,
And wipe out their smile.**

trick

Steal one tile from any opponent's rack without looking.

Opponent does not draw back to 7 tiles until the end of their next turn.

USEFULNESS: 6

When we looked at the "Exchange and still play" card, we said that you should not just change one tile in the hope of picking one specific letter. If you are changing one, it should be when *several* of the letters you might pick will noticeably improve your rack, especially to give you a seven-letter word.

Much the same applies with this card. Don't just steal a tile in the hope of getting a **B** to make **RHUBARB.** But if your rack reads **RETAINA**, which does not make a seven-letter word, and you can't fit in a handy eight-letter word like **REATTAIN** or **MARINATE**, this is the moment to use this card. So many letters combine with **RETAIN** to make a 7 (**CERTAIN**, **PAINTER**, **MINARET**, **TRAINEE** and many more) that you have a high chance of getting a 7-letter word.

As Scrabble Trickster is a new game, it's not surprising there are one or two unclear bits in the rules. It isn't specified, for instance, whether playing seven of the eight tiles you now have after using this card should score you a 50-point bonus. My advice is that playing either seven or all eight tiles should get you the bonus. It's hard enough to get one without making it even more difficult.

Triple word score

**If your score's big or wee,
You can make it times three.**

trick

Triple
Word
Score

USEFULNESS: 8

If you can play this card at the same time as you play a word on an actual Triple Word score square, you get the word tripled and tripled again. A modest score of ten becomes an opponent-flattening 90 points. Or how about this scenario:

Your rack:

You can see you have a **Q** and a **U**, with common letters like E, S and T. With a bit of thought and fiddling with your tiles, you might find an 8-letter word – in this case, **CONQUEST**. With the **Q** on the Double Letter, that scores 29. Now:

TRIPLE IT ONCE for covering the A1 TWS square, making 87.

TRIPLE IT AGAIN for covering the A8 TWS square, making 261.

TRIPLE IT AGAIN if you have the Triple word score card, and now you're up to a gargantuan 783. Add the 50-point bonus, and you've just scored **833** – for one word. All that remains now is to phone the Guinness Book of Records.

While unlikely, a move like this is not entirely unfeasible, which has to propel this card up the usefulness rankings.

Monster Scores

What is the highest score that can be achieved in a game of Scrabble? Nobody knows. Scores of over 1,000 have been made but should be taken with a pinch of salt. A score like that would probably only come about with co-operation from across the table – having a partner rather than an opponent. The other person would have to agree to use as few tiles as possible, and set up lots of nice openings, but not take them.

When Scrabble tournaments were first played in the 1970s and 80s, they were "high score" tournaments. The player with the highest total over however many games was the winner, irrespective of what his or her opponents scored or even who won the games. This meant the game consisted of making openings for high scores, such as putting a tile in an outside row or column to allow high-scoring triple words and even triple-triple words (multiplying your score by nine), and then beating your opponents to them.

Nowadays we play on a "matchplay" basis, meaning you must win your games and win them by as much as possible. Thus you also have to contain your opponent's score, so the high-scoring openings tend not to appear. However, as the dictionary has expanded, and more and more players now study published or computer-generated word lists, scores are as high again now as they were in the old high-score days.

For instance, a potential National Scrabble Champion of a generation ago would have known all the two-letter words and probably the threes, but not all the fours. Today, any player who hopes to win the really big prizes would know all the fours, and some are getting close to knowing the fives as well.

In a social game, about 500 might be a reasonable total score, so you should get 250 against one opponent, about 170 against two, and 125 or so against three. Top players would average about 800, i.e. 400 each (clubs and tournaments only play two-player games).

What about Scrabble Trickster? Some of the cards, especially in combination, have the potential to allow some very high scores indeed. A word on a Triple Word score, using the "Tile normally worth one is worth ten" card, would score maybe 15, tripled to make 45, tripled again if you have a Triple Word score card, making 135 for an ordinary four- or five-letter word.

My guess is that if you generally play three friends and score 125, with Trickster you should look for about 160. Champions who play one other person and usually score 400 should be breaching the 500 barrier quite regularly.

Turn a tile face down and use it as a blank

It's like points in the bank,
Make a letter a blank.

trick

Turn one
of your tiles
facedown and
use it as
a blank.

The blank still
has no value.

USEFULNESS: 9

Good Scrabble players know the value of a blank. No points at face value, but the two blanks are the best tiles in the set. Like the joker at cards, it gives you so much versatility that a 50-point bonus becomes a real possibility.

So clearly this is a very powerful card. Try using each of your tiles as a blank and see if the rack now yields anything useful.

As a little puzzle, try working out the 7-letter word you have with each of the racks below, using this card to turn one letter into a blank in each case:

C₃ E₁ E₁ F₄ N₁ P₃ T₁

A₁ A₁ B₃ D₂ G₂ H₄ I₁

E₁ E₁ E₁ H₄ I₁ O₁ R₁

E₁ F₄ I₁ J₈ L₁ R₁ Z₁₀

If you pick this card, don't waste it. As long as it is not too close to the end of the game, and there is an opening to make a 7-letter word (if there isn't, make one), you should get a bonus within a couple of moves.

That bonus is in there somewhere (probably)

If you struggle to see good words with a blank, try going through the alphabet making it each letter in turn, and see if anything comes to mind. Or look for good combinations: if you have **IN?** (where **?** means a blank), you might be able to make the blank a **G** for an **ING** word. Some people like to move the tiles around on their rack, which can suggest combinations that might not otherwise occur to you.

After a game between strong players, the loser will often excuse his or her defeat by pointing out to the winner that "you got both blanks". Blanks are so important that they will look on getting at least one as almost a prerequisite for winning.

Answers to puzzle on previous page:

PERFECT HANDBAG CHEERIO FRIZZLE

There are some alternative answers, mainly more obscure words. Well done if you got any.

Monster words

We have already mentioned seven and eight-letter words. Is it possible to play even longer words? Certainly. Words up to 15 letters can come about in a number of ways.

Sometimes you can keep adding prefixes and suffixes. If someone played **DOMESTIC**, it could become **DOMESTICATE**, **DOMESTICATED**, and finally **UNDOMESTICATED**.

Or you could do it the other way round. If, say, **UNDER** was on the board, you could extend it to **UNDERINFLATE**, **UNDERCOOKED**, or all manner of other words.

I once managed to convert **SQUANDER** into **SQUANDERMANIA**, a word I dimly remembered. The world champion, New Zealander Nigel Richards, made **REALISMS** into **HYPERREALISMS**. And one of the programs which has been developed for

computer play extended **BASTARD** to
BASTARDISATION.

The least likely way to make a word of this
length would be to play through non-contiguous
letters, i.e. letters not touching each other.
If the top row of a board looked like this:

it could in theory be turned into

This sort of position presenting itself just when
the player had the right tiles, and for the player
to see it, would be so unlikely that a move like
this will probably never be played. The longest
word I have heard of being made like this was
ten letters. But go ahead and try if you want to
be the first to make a fifteen.

Steal an opponent's score

**Your opponent's high scores,
With this card, can be yours!**

trick

**Steal your
opponent's
last score.**

You may still play
a word on your turn.

USEFULNESS: 8

The good thing about this card is there isn't much guesswork involved. You know not to use it when your opponent has just scored three. You do use it when he or she has just scored 53, or 103. How about stealing their 833 when they play **CONQUEST** as a 9-timer with their Triple Word Score card?

Some extra *Trickster* tips

We've already mentioned that it would be worth accepting a lower score to get hold of a couple of those crucial trick cards. There are a few other ways in which *Trickster* differs from normal Scrabble, so let's take a look at a couple of tactics that might help you.

The *Trickster* board

Apart from the trick squares, the other difference between the *Trickster* board and the traditional Scrabble board is the positions of the Premium squares. The eight Triple Word squares are in their familiar places around the outside of the board. The pink centre square is still a Double Word.

There are the same number of Double Word squares (17) and Double Letter squares (24) on both boards. But *Trickster* gives you four extra Triple Letter squares (16 compared to 12).

So it's always worth looking to see if you can get a high scorer like the **Q** or **Z** on a Triple Letter. And don't forget the trick cards, such as making a one-point tile worth ten or the blank worth five; they could combine well with a Triple Letter square to push your score up.

Use more than one premium square in one move

On the opening move a good player, having first checked for a 7-letter bonus, will try to get a high-scoring tile, if they have one, on one of the Double Letter squares. This gets the value doubled, then doubled again as part of a Double Word score.

To do it, you need to find a 5-letter word beginning or ending with the high-scoring tile. But on the *Trickster* board, you only need a 4-letter word, so it may be easier to achieve.

Similarly, where on the normal Scrabble board you need a 5-letter word to stretch from a Triple Letter square to a Double Word (potentially

scoring 60+ with a **Q** or **Z** on the TLS),
with *Trickster*, this again need only be a 4-letter
word.

If you are holding a trick card which again
doubles or triples a word score, or increases
the value of a tile, you could use it along with
a triple-double combination for a very tidy
score indeed.

Keep it a secret

Tournament-standard players are used to doing
something called tile-tracking. This involves
crossing each letter off a prepared grid as it is
played, so that you know what is left at any time
and, in particular, what your opponent is holding
at the end of the game.

Probably no-one is going to take *Trickster* quite
that seriously; and if your opponent plays the
"Turn a tile face down and use it as a blank"
trick card, you won't know what the tile is so
wouldn't be able to track accurately anyway.

But how about, to coin a pleasant-sounding phrase, 'trick-tracking'? It could be useful at the end of a game to know if your opponent might be holding one of the really useful cards, such as using any tile as a blank, stealing an opponent's last score, or cancelling a card. If nothing else, it might warn you to be ready for the psychological blow of having your own high-scoring move cancelled or stolen.

That may also be taking things a bit too seriously; and as all the *Trickster* cards are rarely used in one game, you almost certainly wouldn't know for sure what your opponent(s) is or are holding.

But it is probably worthwhile to keep your cards close to your chest. Nothing in the rules of *Trickster* compels you to read out your trick card when you pick it, so just read it to yourself, turn it upside-down, and be ready to strike with it when the moment is right.

Some *Trickster* puzzles

To see if you are getting the hang of *Scrabble Trickster*, here are a few situations showing you a partly-played game, your rack, and what trick cards you are holding. What would you play in each case?

All the answers are reasonably common words, or words mentioned elsewhere in this book, although you are assumed to know the two-letter words, so keep that card handy if you haven't mastered them yet.

All my answers can be found at the back of this section.

Puzzle 1

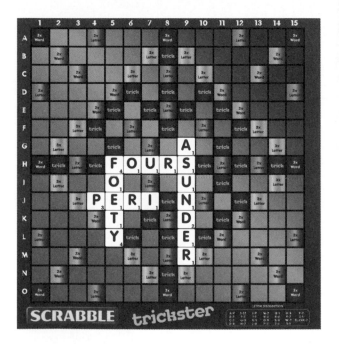

D₂ G₂ I₁ L₁ N₁ P₃ T₁

Cards held:

1. Cancel another player's card.

2. Turn one tile face down and use it as a blank.

3. Score a previously used premium space.

Puzzle 2

98

Cards held:

1. Exchange racks with another player.

2. Play a proper noun.

Puzzle 3

On this board, can you score at least 20 **AND**
get yourself three trick cards with this rack:

A   D   H   I   L   T   W

101

Puzzle 4

	1	2	3	4	5	6	7	8	9	10	11	12	13	14	15
A	3x Word			2x Letter				3x Word				2x Letter			3x Word
B		2x Word				3x Letter	trick	3x Letter						2x Word	
C			2x Word			3x Letter		3x Letter	W₄				2x Word		
D	2x Letter			2x Word	trick		trick		I₁	L₁	2x Letter				2x Letter
E				2x Word	trick		trick	B₃	E₁	L₁	L₁	2x Word			
F			2x Letter	trick			H₄	E₁	A₁	D₂	Y₄		trick	2x Letter	
G		3x Letter			trick		3x Letter	T₁		3x Letter		trick		3x Letter	
H	3x Word	trick	2x Letter	trick		trick	T₁	H₄	O₁	A₁	X₈	trick	2x Letter	trick	3x Word
I		2x Letter			trick		F₄	E₁	N₁		trick			2x Letter	
J			3x Letter	trick		2x Word	O₁		I₁			trick	3x Letter		
K				2x Word	trick		R₁	trick	M₃		trick	2x Word			
L	2x Letter				2x Word	trick	D₂	trick	I₁		2x Word				2x Letter
M			2x Word			3x Letter		3x Letter	S₁			2x Word			
N		2x Word					3x Letter	trick	T₁					2x Word	
O	3x Word			2x Letter				3x Word	S₁	E₁	Z₁₀	I₁	R₁	P₃	

SCRABBLE trickster

C₃ E₁ G₂ I₁ L₁ O₁ R₁

102

Cards held:

1. Triple Word score.

2. Play more than one word in a turn.

3. Blank is worth 5 points.

Puzzle 5

Cards held:

1. Add 10 points to your score.

2. Tile usually worth one point is worth 10.

3. Spell a word anywhere on the board.

Puzzle 6

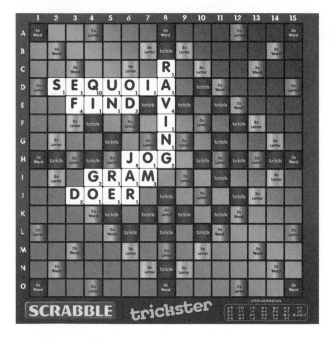

Cards held:

1. Exchange racks with another player.

2. Spell a word backwards.

3. Look at another player's rack of tiles.

Puzzle 7

SCRABBLE *trickster*

A₁ C₃ G₂ H₄ O₁ R₁ S₁

Cards held:

1. Exchange tiles and still play.

2. Steal your opponent's last score.

3. Score a previously used premium space.

Your opponent has just played **GUINEAS** for 92.

Puzzle 8

D₂ N₁ O₁ O₁ U₁ U₁ Z₁₀

110

Cards held:

1. Look at another player's tiles.

2. Score a previously used premium space.

Puzzle 9

Cards held:

1. Add 10 points to your score.

2. Steal a tile from an opponent's rack.

3. Spell a word backwards.

Puzzle 10

Look at this board, and imagine you have each of the racks shown along with the trick card mentioned. Can you score over 100 in each case, using only common words?

EGILQSU and a Triple Word score card.

DEEPLUX and an Add Ten to your Score card.

INRSTTV and a Turn one Tile Face Down and use it as a Blank card.

CEGHINW and a Play Anywhere on the Board card.

CIIKNRT and a Score a Previously Used Premium Space card.

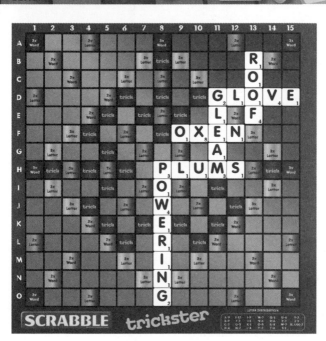

Puzzle 11 - a
Trickster Crossword

Use your *Scrabble Trickster* board to complete this crossword. You will find you cover every trick square on the board and end up with a pleasing pattern. The two-letter words are not clued.

Across
D6 Rental agreement (5)
E7 Agriculture (7)
H2 Light grey colour (5)
H10 Light blue colour (5)
K5 Earth's central line (7)
L6 Bury (5)

Down
F4 Excuse (5)
E5 Small ship (7)
B8 Muscular pain (5)
J8 Sarcastic (5)
E11 Glass worker (7)
F12 Make (someone) laugh (5)

Answers

Puzzle 1

Use the "use a tile as a blank" card to make a word like **PLEDGING** at L7 (72 points). This is better than **PELTING** at A10 as it doesn't give away an easy Triple Word on the top row.

Puzzle 2

Play the proper noun **BEIJING** at M7 for 68.

Puzzle 3

WEALTH at D6 scores 24.

Puzzle 4

Note that someone has used the Spell a Word Backwards card to play **SEZIRP** for a high score.

Playing more than one word in a turn, play **GO** at B9 (12 points), then **RELIC** at A8 (30points), which you triple to 90 with your Triple Word Score card, plus 4 for **EGO**, a total of 106.

An alternative would be **COWGIRL** at C8, scoring 32, again using your Triple Word Score card to make it 96, and hold on to your Play more than one Word in a Turn card.

Puzzle 5

Normally a hopeless rack, the trick cards transform your letters into a gold mine – as long as you remember that handy **EUOI** we mentioned earlier.

Spelling a word anywhere on the board, you play **EUOI** on any corner triple word, such as A1. The tile on the Double Letter square becomes 10 points thanks to the next card, doubled to 20 making 23 for the word. Add another 10 with your last card that makes 33, all tripled, making 99, and add 10 more points for using all three cards. Total – 109 points. Not bad for a terrible rack of letters.

And in case you're wondering, **EUOI** is "an expression of Bacchic frenzy", which means it's what ancient Romans shouted when they were drunk. You might be feeling a bit Bacchic and frenzied yourself with 109 for four vowels.

Puzzle 6

The same board and rack as last time, but different trick cards. With no move worth making, this is the time to exchange racks with another player. If you have more than one opponent, you could use your card to look at the rack of one of them and see if it was worth taking.

Then, with your new and hopefully much improved rack of letters, you might be able to spell a word backwards and get ten extra points for using all three cards. Plus you have stuck your opponent with your lousy rack. You have scored well and made someone unhappy – well done.

Puzzle 7

First, you steal your opponent's score of 92. Then play **CHARS** at D11, also making **STICK**, using your "Score a previously used premium space" card to get the 12 for STICK trebled, for a total of 58 points.

Or you could try using your "Change and still play" card instead. You could change **GHO**, **GOR** or **CGO**, or even just the **O** in the hope of picking an **E** for **CHARGES**, or its interesting anagram **CREAGHS**, a Scottish word for stolen goods. But you might change **GHO** and pick, say, **AII**, leaving you worse off than before, so you should probably hold on to that card until you really need it.

But it's that little steal of 92 that you must make sure you don't miss. That's a swing of 184 between you and him or her. Just don't expect ice-cream for tea if it's your mum.

Puzzle 8

A useful move would be **OUZO** at A6, scoring 38 and gaining a trick card. But placing the O in the top row could leave you open to a big reply by your opponent. They could have the letters for **EXTOLS** from A3, scoring 63, or **QUOTE** at A4 for 72. They could even have a Double Word or Triple Word trick card, to push their score well over 100, maybe 200.

This is the moment to sneak a look at their tiles. If they can't use the opening for much, go ahead. If they have **QUTE** sitting on the rack, look elsewhere for your move, perhaps **OUZO** at J8 for 27 or L9 for 28, or just **ZO** at C6, which scores 36 but keeps the awkward duplicate **U**'s.

There is a danger they could have the "Tile usually worth one is worth ten" trick card, in which case they could play any 5-letter word through your **O**, scoring 70+, if you play at A6. But sometimes you have to take a chance in life, and it's never a good idea to play ultra-defensively just in case an opponent has some particular tile or card. Strike a balance between playing your own rack and not giving away something silly.

Puzzle 9

The key thing to notice here is you are close to a 50-point bonus. Don't be tempted to play **LADIES** at D12 for 28 and two trick cards.

Instead, steal a tile from your opponent (your strongest opponent, if you have more than one). Lots of letters go with **LADIES** to make a 7-letter word, such as **DENIALS**, **MISLEAD/MISDEAL**, **DETAILS/DILATES**, **DAILIES/LIAISED**, **BALDIES/DISABLE**, **DERAILS/REDIALS**, **LADDIES**, **SALLIED** and some more obscure stuff like **EYLIADS** (glances or winks), **SKAILED** (dispersed), and **DEISEAL**, **DEASOIL** and **DEASILS**, all of which refer to sunwise motion. Any 7-letter word you get will fit in down column 12.

If you get, say, an **M**, you could use your other card to spell **MISLEAD** or **MIDSDEAL** backwards, making it cover two Double Word squares thus getting it quadrupled. With the "add 10 points to your score" card (before counting the Double Word score), you would get ten for the word, plus ten for the card making 20, quadrupled making 80, 14 for **TZARS** making 94, plus ten for using three trick cards is 104, and the 50-point bonus making 154. Plus three new trick cards to replenish your stock.

Puzzle 10

SQUIGGLE at O3 plus card scores 137.

EXPEL at A11 plus card scores 106.

Use the card to make your **V** an **E** and play **INTEREST** at A15 for 113.

CHEWING anywhere on a Triple Word score and with the **H** or **W** on a Triple Letter square scores 110.

TRICKING at O1 scores 104.

Puzzle 11

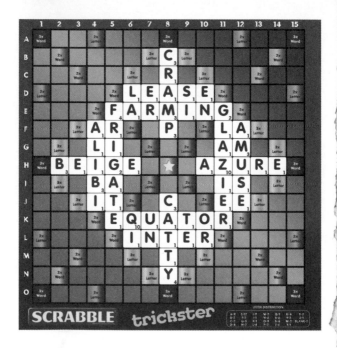